REVEILLE

REVEILLE

POEMS BY GEORGE DAVID CLARK

The University of Arkansas Press
Fayetteville
2015

ISBN: 978-1-55728-674-1
eISBN: 978-1-61075-559-7

19   18   5   4   3   2

Designed by Ellen Beeler

⊛ The paper used in this publication meets the minimum requirements
of the American National Standard for Permanence of Paper for Printed
Library Materials Z39.48-1984.

Library of Congress Control Number: 2014949933

Acknowledgments

Grateful acknowledgment is made to the editors of the books and periodicals in which these poems previously appeared, often in earlier versions and under different titles: *Alaska Quarterly Review,* "Denouement in a Wooden Dollhouse"; *Antioch Review,* "White Noise"; *The Believer,* "Prodigalia: Lionhide"; *Blackbird,* "The Past a Sanctuary Staffed by Poltergeists"; *Cimarron Review,* "Matches"; *Copper Nickel,* "Reveille with Reimbursement" and "Whatever Burn This Be"; *Cream City Review,* "The Picture of Little G. C. in a Prospect of Flowers"; *FIELD,* "Heimlich for a Heavenly Windpipe"; *Greensboro Review,* "Lullaby with Bourbon"; *Missouri Review,* "Reveille with Lullabies"; *Narrative Magazine,* "Python in a Grand Piano," "Prodigalia: Trident and Leviathan," and "Born Blind, Discipled by the Blue"; *New Millennium Writings,* "Heimlich for a Heavenly Windpipe" reprint; *Pleiades,* "Interview Conducted through the Man-Eater's Throat" and "Prodigalia: Cashmere and Meerschaum"; *Quarterly West,* "Reveille with Kazoo"; *Redux: A Literary Journal,* "Whatever Burn This Be" and "Variations on Her Bed in Shadows" reprints; *River Styx,* "Variations on Her Bed in Shadows"; *Salt Hill,* "Reveille on a Silent Whistle"; *Shenandoah,* "A Stipulation"; *Southern Humanities Review,* "Cradles"; *Southern Poetry Review,* "Jellyfish," "The Past as a Public Swimming Pool," and "Love Parade"; *Stirring: A Literary Collection,* "Reveille with Kazoo," "Reveille with Reimbursement," and "Reveille on a Silent Whistle" reprints; *Yale Review,* "Cigarettes."

"A Stipulation" was also published online at *Poetry Daily.* "Jellyfish" and "Lullaby with Bourbon" appeared at *Verse Daily.* "Matches" and "Jellyfish" were reprinted in *Improbable Worlds* (Mutabilis Press, 2012). "Matches" also appeared as a broadside in collaboration with the artist Meghan Keane (Broadsided Press, 2012) and in *The Southern Poetry Anthology, Vol. VI: Tennessee* (Texas Review Press, 2013). "Interview Conducted through the Man-Eater's Throat" and

"Prodigalia: Cashmere and Meerschaum" appeared in *The Emma Press Anthology of Homesickness and Exile* (The Emma Press, 2014). "Python in a Grand Piano" was reprinted in *New Poetry of the Midwest* (New American Press, 2014).

Thanks to Mike Bieker, David Scott Cunningham, Melissa King, Tyler Lail, and everyone at the University of Arkansas Press.

Thanks to Enid Shomer, editor of editors, and to the other editors whose insight improved these poems in manuscript or who championed the work with special recognition, especially Carol Edgarian, Tom Jenks, Dominic Luxford, Kathrine Nuernberger, and James Smith.

Thanks to the institutions that provided me with support and employment during the years in which these poems were written and revised: University of Virginia, James Madison University, Texas Tech University, Colgate University, and Valparaiso University.

Thanks to my teachers and mentors: Peter Balakian, Curtis Bauer, Rita Dove, Jacqueline Kolosov, Gregory Orr, Bobby C. Rogers, Lisa Russ Spaar, William Wenthe, Charles Wright, and especially John Poch.

Thanks to Dorothy Bass, Betsy Burow-Flak, Joe Creech, Mary Beth Fletcher, Peter Kanelos, Mike Owens, Mark Schwehn, Kathy Sutherland, Sandra Visser, and everyone affiliated with the Lilly Fellows Program.

And thanks to the fellow writers who have advanced my poems with their insight, friendship, and encouragement, especially Aaron Alford, Lauri Anderson, Jasmine V. Bailey, Evan Beaty, Brian Brodeur, Joseph Chapman, Henrietta Goodman, Julia Hansen, Lilah Hegnauer, Adam Houle, Christine Kitano, Derek McKown, Jake Ricafrente, John Schneider, Michael Shewmaker, Justin Sider, Amber Stamper, and Mark Wagenaar.

Most of all, thanks to Elisabeth, my one and only.

Contents

No was the night. Yes is this present sun.

—*Wallace Stevens*

REVEILLE

REVEILLE ON A SILENT WHISTLE

Two seraphs in the live oak's highest boughs are sleeping,
constructing minutely their crystalline fretwork,

a lattice of musics: the inscrutable curios of angels
in the holy bottegas of their dreams. One conceives

a rope of braided sand, fabrics made wholly of water,
what will never exist. The other is drafting a likeness

of God, whom she has met only once, and then simply
as a void in her manifold and involute consciousness.

Dawn comes and like reflections on the rain-pocked surface
of a pond the creatures dissolve beyond a curtain of brilliance,

the wake their Lord casts moving between one state
and another. Rising there, from what we might foolishly

call a slumber but is in fact a kind of distant prayer
unto Himself, He forgets them, or better, sacrifices them

to the shade of His lesser attentions. What He remembers,
what He continues, carefully, to imagine—projecting it now

through these gauzy drapes dappled by sun and leaf-shadow,
into this very bedroom—is the instant of your waking,

Sleeper, the moment when even before a first thought flickers,
your being purls and quickens as though something good

had breathed on you. Listen: that's your singular name
unfurling through the whisper-weight trumpets of light.

JELLYFISH

The dark sea dreams them.
They are the unexchangeable
currency of dreams,

the interest the other world
pays and pays into this one.
In the pre-dawn blue

they seem hewn out
from the littoral like great
waterlogged diamonds,

an interior gleam.
Who speaks for them
speaks for the secret

side of the womb,
for they are the long-tasseled
death-bonnets of children

we conceive but never
bring to term. And so we love
and jointly curse them.

It is impossible now
to tell if they reach for us
or we for them, so strange

is their volatile gravity.
They are sisters
to the moon then, and pulse

in her wake, a curdled
blooming of echoes
as she too is an echo.

But in the fluorescent pink
and green pockets
of their bodies, softer

than night, they're smuggling
rumors of suns we fail
to imagine. They hold

whole oceans above
their umbrellas. Tell me,
friend, is there an end

to revelation? The poison
flowers blossom inside us
like Rorschachs

we might believe in.
Evening and thunderheads
in the austral sky,

the jellyfish tides,
an exhibition of lightnings
and scaled-down Hiroshimas:

if they proceed
like messengers,
another breed of angel,

then it falls on us to hear
and heed them,
their cold medusa-bells

resounding, calling us
back through the black
sand of sleep.

THE PAST AS A PUBLIC SWIMMING POOL

The lifeguard is ever nineteen and pretty
in a bathing suit red as tomatoes.
The swim team plows the green fields
of chlorine, then plows them again.

Only the air changes. With our approach
the mercury spikes in the neck
of the glass thermometer that hangs
beside a clock at the concessions stand,
and when we touch the outer gate, navy chevrons
on the vinyl chaises fairly twitch
in the sun's kaleidoscope. Pop on the radio
and beneath it the almost audible sizzle
of high school girls tanning, bronze
and bronze. Yellow jackets in the mouth
of a coke can. Any closer and we'd cook.

Such terrible faithlessness in a high dive—
rampant monument to the next-in-line.
Now and always would-be caryatids
wait their chance to briefly pose
between the spring board and the sky.

PYTHON IN A GRAND PIANO

Beneath the gloss
of lacquered walnut,
golds and olives
jigsaw. Muscle
and musk. Dust motes
in suspension.
Lengths of leaf-
and loam-colored
scales in wreaths
above the soundboard
like music at rest.
How a trailing silence
sometimes tricks us
into thinking
that a tune's released
its cincture on
the room. We fold
the sheets of Chopin,
see them vanish
in the bench. But
quiet doesn't
free us. Something
rasps and gathers
in the dark parts
of an open ear:
reticulated thunder,
yard on yard
melodic rope.
The score, we find,
is longer than

it seems and stronger.
To catch the thing
that knots us we
sit down and bait
the keys. Relax
and watch the parlor
grand digest
the small white mice
that were our hands.

CRADLES

Honeysuckle taught me the nose
     is a cradle. Her brown breasts
teach me the yellow-lace bra.

    Altars consume what they elevate—
their praise is a column of smoke—
       but even the most indelicate cradles

anchor their freights as they raise them.
     The firelight cast on the antler-mount
cleaves to a hammock of bone.

    We laurel an athlete's skull with a helmet,
and the femme fatale's heels
      in stilettos perch there like regents

in thrones. When it blows
     some cradles rock and yaw in the wind.
Some vessels fuse to their payloads.

    Who can say if it's stars that cradle
the zodiac, or constellations
      the stars; her lips the kiss or vice versa.

I know a cradle that keeps out the dark
     and a cradle that is the dark too.
The moon in the pond. Dry seas

    on the moon. The tiered chandelier
and the lampshade. Skin but not skin,
      the amputee's scars cradle what's left

11

of the elbow. The age-deafened ear
          makes a cradle for quiet. And, hurried,
my stutter still dandles hard letters

          as though they were fragile
and loved. It's clear to me now,
          the cradles of language that tether

the mind will each come undone
          if I touch them, collapse their bright
comas to bedsores and time.

          Some noon an altar will lift me,
but this morning I want to be kept
          the way that a well keeps its pillar

of shadow, this gossamer obelisk
          built to dissolve, but not yet.
O cups on their saucers, cream

          in the coffee. For a cradle of favor,
see the small of her back. The backs
          of her knees for guile. I'd love her

out loud, but her intricate silence
          says the tongue is an altar,
and she's cradled my name

          in her mouth for a while.

HEIMLICH FOR A HEAVENLY WINDPIPE

Like ice-cold cola in its transit through a plastic straw
sometimes a pleasure enters him, and after a smooth
drafting down the spine, issues from his leg,
the crippled one he drags behind him,
the one sunk to its ankle in an angel's mouth.
Spaghetti negro at the beach café in Positano,
for instance, with the bougainvillea tinting the breeze
purple in the avenues that scale the hill.
Or that refrain of Roethke's and Samantha quoting it
to mean she'd like to rest a little longer on the chaise
in her bikini. Fall in the Blue Ridge, Technicolor fall.

Occasionally though, the angel chokes on something.
Standing on the porch at the propane grill
with whisky in his coke and skirt steaks cooking,
the man hears a motorcycle fire up in the alley,
knows it wakes the baby and the vegetables inside
will be delayed. This, the first warm night
in April. Small and larger hardships marble it
with fat, gristle. And now the angel gags.
If the man's annoyed by what's become a ritual—
the holy face plum-colored, sputtering—
still eventually he stoops and lifts the creature up:
difficult because its wings are huge
and clenched in spasms. When at last they part,
he stands between them, joins his hands,
and jerks back hard under the supple ribcage
till the clot's dislodged. Dry coughs, then furious
breathing. Milky feathers scattered on the porch
and in his cola. And the angel already kneeling,
unhinging its jaw for more.

LOVE PARADE

The heartthrobs ferrying Miss Universe
on a lacquered palanquin fly streamers

from their naked shoulders,

and blow their kisses also to the crowds.
Between the penthouse balconies

noon burnishes a fleet of cartoon giants

filled with helium, pours
ponds of shade over the puppeteers

who soak below like fishing lures.

The marching bands have drunk
such pleasure, they're spewing

confetti wherever they go.

Baton twirlers on roller skates.
Floats dressed in live butterflies.

And while saints-to-be throw chocolates

from the backs of pachyderms,
I roll around the corner

in the car we first kissed in.

The paintjob's a roaring canary
and that's pink champagne in my hand.

CIGARETTES

It's August, hot, and a newly-married
couple in Mobile have left the window
partly open to the night and road noise
while they make love on a futon in the dark.
After, as he breathes heavy on the pillow
beside her and a thin clear string of semen
seems to quiver on the white guitar
that is her belly, she sighs and says,
Oh, now I wish I had a cigarette.

He's been thinking he should pull the sheet
from where it's bunched along the floor
and it takes him a moment to understand
that cigarettes—which both of them detest
and she has never tried—are not her point.
She phrases it that way because pleasure
is complicated, more so perhaps than suffering.
It will augment and diminish, both,
not unlike the ancient priests who'd purge
the humid entrails of the pharaohs
and then bathe the bodies' cavities
with myrrh and frankincense and palm wine,
freights of fragrance in the hollows after.
She means that monuments to rapture
should be light to carry and combustible,
toxic in small quantities even secondhand,
and with an odor that darkens one's clothes.

Somehow he comprehends this vaguely.
It reminds him of a concert he attended

in high school, the massive outdoor stage
where the band played one encore, a second,
then mangled their guitars across the amps
and footlights: sparks, debris, electric howling.
Stoned and riding home with his ears fuzzing
in the back of a friend's Topaz, he felt
invincible and fantasized a car crash.
He'd passed out then, and later, coming to
sore-throated and coughing on his parent's porch
where the guys had left him, it was as though
some breakneck song—all glass and metal
in his mind—had wrecked around him.
He rose there slowly and limped out of it
the way a man emerges from a shattered
windshield, the live adrenaline already
funneling off, but with a few stray echoes
still looping through his chest like feedback.

Tonight on the far side of the room
the infinite lungs of the wall clock exhale
long gray minutes. Eyes shut, motionless,
his wife leans toward sleep. Her teeth
are tingling faintly, white but crooked
on the bottom row. She has clenched
and ground them during sex again
and now she guesses at the likelihood
of braces in her future when there's money.
It is her habit to sweep the tender downside
of her tongue across the misalignments
where the frets of wire might someday run,
and for a moment her mouth becomes
the smoky back room in a downtown bar
where a struggling band from out-of-state
is just about to plug in their Les Pauls.

Nascent music crackles in the outlets,
jittering, almost perceptibly, the ashtrays.

A breeze sleepwalks the curtains back
into the room and out again. Back and out.
Her husband slides his heel along her calf
and starts to tell her they should set his legs
on fire (she could inhale while they kiss),
but no, she's gone unconscious. Instead,
he pulls the sheet to their shoulders
and thinks, as he dissolves beside her,
how from a distance they would look like two
thin cylinders wrapped in white, their minds
these grainy filters in their heads. Asleep
before he gets to who might smoke them
and why, his breathing slows and deepens.
The room cools slightly. The traffic
lulls outside and the sex aroma dissipates
till only the air that cycles through their chests
is warmed and sonorous and redolent.

REVEILLE WITH KAZOO

From your overlong, even invincible sleep;
from the pink and orange moth-scales
that collect on your mind like a dust;
from the stately plush where you jonah
in a bottled frigate's belly;
from this lopsided aerie of marigold sheets:
wake up.
                  Sleeper, your shoelaces knot
out of boredom. Light wants in your pockets
like money. Wake up from the torpors
of cat fur, from these lingerie dragnets
of lace. The swimming pools
of the future were born this morning
and tenderly swaddled in sun-lust.
Pamphlets announcing new flavors
of ice cream descend on the plaza
in a blitz of sugar. And under the bridge
an angel spray-paints her wings.

INTERVIEW CONDUCTED THROUGH THE MAN-EATER'S THROAT

Are you in there, friend?

Like the blue-black char in a chimney.
If I crane my neck at the windpipe's flue,
I can see a far sky framed
in teeth, a double horseshoe
of mauve lips, and there's your face
bent toward my trouble. I'm the fresh inch
of ash in the furnace,
a twist of smoke where the stack is bent.

What happened to you, friend?

My whole life happened. I was napping
by an open window, sun
on my back through mosquito netting
while a hired boy strummed
the guitar. For a long time nothing
happened. Then a chord went wrong.
I felt a shadow and turned to a knifing
smile that devoured my yawn.

Friend, friend, were you taking precautions?

I slaughtered clean goats on an altar
of antlers, gave Caesar's
to Caesar, remembered my psalter.
I installed a procedure
for the watchmen's patrols: their whistles

were nickel, they carried red beacons.
Each guard wore a sword and a pistol.
I swore I was safe, and yet, I was eaten.

Friend, what happened?

The great maw happened
and the rough red tongue.
Now this little room happens
where a lantern's hung
above a small square desk
and wicker stool that squat
by the throbbing wall. There's a flask
and matches on a blistered cot.

The beast is sleeping. Can you climb out, friend?

Past those teeth in their ivory
rows, the gash of gums,
those livid tonsils? Even if I dared, every
time he coughs my grip comes
free in offal. And before you ask, that fiery
sinkhole in the corner is worse. It flexes
and sparks: an acid catalogue, a diary
in gastric stinks. These are not exits.

Well, what are your plans, friend?

I believe I'm meant to wait at the table.
I'll sample the whisky and host
this little lottery that's straddled
on the monster's gut. The roasted
stool wants company. I'll play a solitaire
that contemplates the well-gnawed

rubble for a sign: how a prayer
busies itself between the ears of God.

Friend, what is that noise?

Outside, you can hear that rumbling?
He's waking up and he's hungry.
That noise wants empires tumbling
down a throat. It's the jangling
of relics in a pocket of lung and I'm coming
to understand it. I'm not angry
now or even scared. I think something's
being chewed on that will change me.

A STIPULATION

"I speak to the unbeautiful of this bird . . . "

If a group of peacocks is,
                          collectively, an ostentation,
a flock of peahens might be aptly termed a what?
A penury? Humiliation?
                          Even they—in sepias
(but for their brief green collars), backs matte gray

with speckled under-feathers—preen and strut.
We may know that seven peahens in a shagbark is a pity,
a brownout,
                    but the four dusting themselves at length
along the driveway, let's call them
                                    a stipulation:

vanity has never been reserved for classic beauties,
the body wants to be a temple
                          to no god but itself.

PRODIGALIA

Cashmere and Meerschaum

When I first furnished my suite in the city,
I had a cashmere hammock
slung between the tusks of a tremendous elephant
whose bust was mounted on the bedroom wall.
In that prodigious net young ladies
from the delta used to tumble like rabbits.
I could feel their hearts,
like rabbits', beating through their chests,
and imagine, with some encouragement,
that I was God.

And there was too the elephant himself:
the leather blankets of his ears
that I'd detach to draw around my shoulders
while I slept; the hidden drawer
inside his trunk that held my meerschaum pipe
and petty cash; the eye marbles—
color of a low gas flame—
through which he glowered at me
his great suspicion, and, now and then,
flashed forth a look of obliterating tenderness
not unlike a father's.

Lionhide

Evenings on the Street of Ermine
men with silver find a brothel
where the comely whores on pedestals
are dressed in leaves or feathers:
one's made up to be a peacock,
one an ibis, one flamingo,
one with blossoms on her wrists
is June magnolia, one is ginkgo.

For no small cost a tailor
in Akkah takes custom orders,
then from fowl or flora sews
the girls their ornate wardrobes.
I hired his skill for bedclothes
made to terrify from lion hide:
tawny flanks, a copper loin,
paw pads blue as cyanide.

With the russet mane combed back
like a collar and that shock of hair
at tail tip styled into a teardrop,
I preyed on ostrich in their boudoir
caves and slept in the boughs
of a flowering almond. My claws
at love were lethal, and the way
they'd flay a gown, then pause

above a jugular, left me breathless
in the lion's head, and hungry,
panting on the brink of slaughter.
Nights, I mastered a leonine carriage,
taught my lungs passable roars.

By day, polite in genteel villas,
I jawed with chatelaines in jaguar
boots and mufflers of chinchilla.

How I went savage was civilized
and slow. Safaris ran counter
to my neighbors' dreams of towers
in the city of iron, but I could sleep-talk
metal for hours, thinking fur and fronds
and feathers all the while. My fattened
lusts, like muscles, hurt from flexing,
and they liked to hurt, to madden.

When a moon that reeked of jasmine
sent me growling after owlet twins
with snowy breasts and flecks
of silver peppered on their skin,
I kissed and licked and bit them
at the shoulders, pelves, wrists.
And when they screamed, I set my canines
in their throats and with two twists

had quit them. I left by a frosted window
with blood in my mane, and saw
a man in goat-hair lapping sewage
from a gutter, an oak limb
dressed in rope for someone's hanging.
The eastern hills flushed pinot noir
and shop fronts blued reflective
till I made every glass I passed an abattoir.

Trident and Leviathan

The merchant Syrian who sold it
claimed whoever slept there dreamed
as gods dream, in unearthly colors
unmoored from scene and sequence;
that a sleeper in the bed of beds
was sometimes Neptune, sometimes Jonah
thrown with pleasant company into a buoyant rest;
that in an aqueous slumber prayers
are magnified and echo till you know not
whether you are speaking or being spoken to.

Installed, the king-size cypress frame
stood five feet high, required a gangplank
to be boarded, but the marvel was the mattress
filled with water: an oceanscape
beneath transparent plastic, lit softly from below
and stocked with purple cichlids, angelfish,
and a moray eel who liked to hide himself
among the turquoise knots of coral.

While the courtyard palms were buffeted
in windstorm and all Babylon scuttled in dust,
the effects of water forked by lamplight
shot my walls in silver prisms.
Nested aquarium, womb, lunar oasis
at the nexus of noons: I slept
but never dreamed there.
Nor did I, in that fluid twilight, feel the need
to court a god. No one prays
who's prayed to. When I'd remove the cap
and scatter wafers, fish would lavish
wet oblations out their gills. Even the moray

eyed me like an idol. Whole days I'd lie
suspended in their sky to watch them
track my hands like heavens.

Then the solstice fevered through me.
I let the lamp under the bed burn low.
My mind clouded and the mattress fogged.
Through the blear the moray's gaze unnerved me.
The fish would stir the bed and seemed inspired
to curse me with a host of pointed leers
aimed right into my resting. If I closed my eyes,
I'd fall through bedding like ejected ballast.
The great eel snapped his jaw. I could still nap
sometimes in fitful snatches, but would shortly
jerk awake as though Sleep herself
had gagged and spat me out.

WHITE NOISE

The sound of the self, or the self's deletion?

Like wind tossing leaves of aluminum foil,

Sun-babble cooling in swirls of moon dust.

A sterilized music, a soothing unreason.

* * *

An atomized god, or a god's accretion?

The mind's swimming laps in Styrofoam peanuts,

In the latest decrees from the caucus of cretins.

Like birdsong in nightmare. The boiling of seas.

* * *

That sandpaper rasping of grief on grief:

Lobotomy's soundtrack, the curdle of semen.

We've amplified fog and made audible bleach.

The sound of our names in the dialect of demons.

THE PICTURE OF LITTLE G. C. IN A PROSPECT OF FLOWERS

Beyond the hill a gathering
of eggplant-grays is fraught
with volts and lathering
while background elms blow taut
and molten in the spill.

Seeming almost to admire
the child among them, these blossoms nod
their puny lightning rods
and lean toward his lap
like fingers to a fire.

They are not real flowers though.
They're flytraps
with open mouths
so petal-pink they echo
orchids in their blowze.

The year-old boy in overalls
and ball cap squinches
up his face to caterwaul
and mauls away
at the anthology of pinches.

He has no history to keep
him calm before a throng
of rabid hazards. He's just a child.
The winds are strong. The hill is steep
and the perspective long.

DENOUEMENT IN A WOODEN DOLLHOUSE

Attention, Dollhouse, to the sound of stage drapes
furling back and a soft snap
                              almost like the striking
of a match. That easily you're lit: one lick
and then a flicker at the paisley couch—
the balsa floor lamp blooming like a tulip,
while the chandelier shivers and flares then pops
its glass piñata
                    to spit firedrops through the room.

Groomdoll, if each chair is cotton stuffing
in a cufflink box—if tissue—then you knew day one
you lived in kindling,
                         but what else could you do?
The work of dolls
                    is small-scale drama,
but with no director and no plot, you mostly labored
at the hallway mirror, practicing extremes of feeling
on your plastic face. Here's the horror you perfected.

Bridedoll, as a host of crackling yellows
climbs the spiral stairs behind you, something
in your hollow parts is warming toward a climax.
What or who
              have you been miming? How awful much
of you is costume? Singed in your retreat and torn,
your gown has let a little air in,
                                    and the aria you're always
on the verge of rises in you like a vow that's been inverted.

Attention, Dolls: your immolation's imminent.
Already something's at the door to the master bedroom,
is painting it red, will soon lacquer it black.
I've been so lonely, someone says.

                                    I know,
the other answers. With that, the dialogue stalls.
You touch,

                    and then you're burning. Somewhere,
past the flimsy panels, you can almost hear applause.

REVEILLE WITH REIMBURSEMENT

Sleep is a flat tax. Everyone pays it.
Closing our eyes, we open
like wallets.

                        * * *

In a lost hour ants scale the leg of a table
and march toward a bowl of oranges.
If I tracked the dotted line across the hardwood,
down the hall, I'd see that black cortege
trail back over your pillow, one ant and another
from the whiteness of your ear.

                        * * *

On the deck at three A.M.
I saw chimneys siphon bats
from a velvety heaven where the governors
count our debts out on an abacus of satellites.

Let the tax collectors come
if they can find us. Shake the nightcap
of ants from your hair.
I've brought you the orange you dreamed of.

BORN BLIND, DISCIPLED BY THE BLUE

The water's color came to me
the way that music does a deaf man
with his hands on the piano's rim.

Now I know how I'd been parched
past conscious thirsting.
I'd hear a trickle and I'd stare,

intent at nothing.
I felt braver than a riptide
in the bathtub's warm asylum—

bolder almost than a shark tank—
but at the rush of natural cobalt
I could be counted on to balk

and shudder. Immersion meant
another blindness, loosed the feeling
from my limbs. So I wouldn't let

the local river with its snowmelt currents
soak me. Still, I liked to fall asleep
where I could launch my mind

like baited fishline from a bridge.
A couple times I woke up panicked
from the torque of liquid turquoise

till the dream simmered off
and I found myself dry. Traumas, yes:
but, friend, they thrilled me, drilled

slippery corkscrews brilliant
through my eyes. The tint
I glimpsed was half acceleration

and another third of it was ice.
The rest I couldn't put a name on.
After that—I didn't plan it,

but along the vacant beach
I waded in one February evening,
surf roiling all around me

and my denim strange
with saturated weight. One swell
and then another, like a careful

wildness, bent to lift me.
My breath left. I stumbled, lost
my legs, and then was struck

and struck by breakers till I floundered
and the salt shot holes through
all my sense. Might just as easily

have drowned there, but washed back
against the shore with my skin
at every facet prickling,

I knew I'd fairly choked on icy
color, held its shiver in my hands.
Since that night, my eyes,

each a compass, always spin
to quickest winter, to the chill
thrust through the center of the blue.

VARIATIONS ON HER BED IN SHADOWS

1.

The pair of ivory pens
inside their velvet case
are black. The flash
of carving knives is cancelled
when they're drawered.
The woman's legs go
dark between the sheets.

2.

Night's fractures make her bed
a jigsaw puzzle
in a thousand pieces. Nearly all
describe the folds of her duvet.
In those remaining
find an ankle and an earlobe.
Then fit the scene together
with your eyes closed.

3.

From the doorknob
her jaguar pajamas,
like an empty pelt, hang.
She the hunter intrepid,
she the animal slain.

4.

Streetlight and venetian blinds.
A study of lines: the way the yellow
slats proceed by level rungs

over the nightstand, the way they dip
and swerve across her hips.

5.

Forget the long white fangs
drawn back in a cottonmouth;
for a stay of lethal fleetness,
see her legs relaxed
between the sheets.

6.

When the pied
horizon lightens
and the entourage
of umbras disperse,
they leave behind
this shadow thrown
across the footboard
like a fur-lined coat,
these grays that slip
like coins into the settee,
and this little clutch
of darkness tucked
beneath her arm.

7.

What do we divine
by these two deviants,
her long pale legs
in their veil
of linen? The bed's
a clock gone haywire
or a compass
locked on heaven.

WHATEVER BURN THIS BE

he had first a little cold so began to cough
then could not stop coughing could not
even at night willing the throat relaxed
while his wife sought rest beside him stop

as though there were a magician and this act
called for him to draw a chain of brightly-
colored handkerchiefs from out a humbled gullet
the itch of it the steady need in waves

to cough and somehow the handkerchiefs
continuing long after any ordinary feint
had been completed at the clinics coughing yet
while doctors snaked their special cameras

through his nose and raw esophagus
that high-tech scrutiny for polyps finding none
no profit from the chest exams
ditto prescription salves inhalers steroids weeks

and months of treatments with referrals each
to new physicians likewise confident
and ineffectual until what had seemed
some misdirection of contagion

then resembled more a sorcery
a kind of violent miracle and under
escalating cost and wrack of spasm
he commenced then dubiously begging

that a god he didn't half-believe existed
would touch with healing hand this throat
where the whole world's droughts were local
extinguish now whatever unslaked burn this be

he rasped his pleas aloud would sleep
and dream of coughing wake to coughing
and in hours closed to anything but thought
and coughing he imagined himself

magistrate among the scalded throats
of Mexico the boys expectorating fire
for tourists till the inevitable night
that flash they spit they swallow

too he dwelt on Colombian neckties
desecration whereby throats are opened
and the tongue jerked down jerked
throbbing forth to dry like suffering's ascot

would think romantically of a torturer's
garrote the metal coolness on an Adam's apple
even as the victim choked and more
cruel still he dreamed himself

hauled out on stage by this magician-sadist
his body locked from the neck down
in a rough wood box while whetted coughs
like saw blades slit and split him

who he wondered watched this
from the soundless gallery he couldn't see
for heaven clearly to his slow sere prayers
was silent just as he foreknew it would be

and further yet despairing then
he entertained the staid analysis
of certain liquid suicides a meditation
on the image of a man relaxing poolside

in the ruthless prime of summer
with a sweating glass of antifreeze
or the slow black drip of motor oil
into the grinding cog-works of his chassis

saw such tonics more like spells
or counter-curses by which he might pit
cough vs industry and all the best
combustion human beings have devised

he spit goddamn and now he meant it
O could not stop this ceaseless Santa Ana
within his precious windpipe chambered
so he coughed and cursed

gave in to coughing lavished
in that millisecond fraction of relief inside
each cough like thimble-shots of nectar
in a cactus coughed though surely each balm

broke on deeper coughing no longer spoke
but croaked or hissed poor throat scoured
throat blistered flayed excoriated throat
and still in addition to prescription-everything

tried homemade syrups tried honey tried
lemon-rose-holy-spring-and-salt water
a couple times counter-intuitive bouts
of better whiskies tried tequila with chilled

V-8 chasers tried to sandblast the throat
and start again from nothing always bags
of mentholated lozenges always ice-cold
carbonated anything and yet the constant

curdle of his larynx such that finally knee-wise
bent again for supplication half-swearing
half-whispering like carnal secrets his appeals
for simple peace to pain itself

mindlessly whimpering there for draught
of anything to ease this long red rash
of perfect coughing then
then like someone finally told the story

of a scar they'd worn since infancy
his cough seemed simultaneously more
and less a myth and he began suspecting
as his thoughts turned odd he might at last

be hearing a reply that if transcendent coughs
like his existed so must god a god
much stranger than he'd guessed that maybe
angled properly the noise he made

this ultimate ugliness could strike the ears
of paradise in a way no prayer could hope to
that to soothe a genius cough like his
he might start thinking like a throat

an instrument of coughing he might
become a smarter kind of cough
productive of something curiously beautiful
ordained a consecrated cougher who

by saint-like coughing harder with more pure
hurt behind it might cough up the cure
for something cough precious stones or cough .
a beam of whole white light cough out

the worst parts of himself until he was
another man entirely revival fire
and brimstone coughing gospel coughing
on a stage to wild amens coughing to end

wars and famines and coughing too to call
the necessary rain lakes of it cataracts
and pearly Caribbeans of deluge coursing
blessedly the cool blue throat of an evening sky

could a new cough clean him
could he be sanctified by long apocalyptic
coughing would hurt men come to him
asking meekly that he please cough for them

cough please over them so god might
through him hear their own hidden
and inarticulate hackings voiced the way
they felt them that the lord might disburse

his mercy please sir cough they'd softly say
and moved he would in thick bellowing fits
of messianic coughing cough for them
cough kindly over them throw back his head

and let go coughs like a magician's
plump white doves an endless stream in flight
toward heaven that cracked and ragged
blessing through his crimson throat forever

MATCHES

Red-faced, arguing briefly
their one point against the night,

or blackened, sober as blown
light bulbs, they weigh more

in the eye than the hand.
Infernal dragonflies,

their wings pinched off.
Informal flames on crutches.

I work the fresh match
like a needle to sew a gown

of blue fire for the chandelier.
I grip the spent match

like a pen, signing my soot
to this debt and that one.

The matches' testament—
which includes the diary

of an arsonist's slender apprentice,
her virginity like a fistful

of tinder—is the history of glory
in the language of ash.

They stutter, and still
they are eloquent.

THE PAST A SANCTUARY STAFFED BY POLTERGEISTS

The tireless editors of ecclesial design
have rearranged the vestments in the closets
of your mind, and now it's lousy paisley
couches cruising through the anterooms,
the transepts' saintly portraits upside down.
Most icons in the attics have already been
forgotten into boxes marked with gibberish,
the calligraphy of ghosts. There's that squeal
like magic markers on cardboard sometimes—
faint, but your whole skull shivers: one more
bit of memoir, just the nimbus of a headache,
locked away or tumbled down your spine.

Surprising where you find a sacred fragment,
when you find one in the present.
Among the clammy delicates you transfer
to a dryer, maybe: *junior high with the cool feel
of a phone cord coiled around your little finger.*
Or once, in your husband's kiss, *leaf-scent
fragrant in a sweatshirt,* as he held you in the wake
of several whiskeys. Incense on his tongue,
and then his mouth like marshmallows
and chocolates by a bonfire. Each kiss after
there was less of it. Only lips by morning.

You might think the poltergeists are cruel.
They hide the antiques one by one and dim
the white you were inside your first bikini.
They steal your mother's fondness for azaleas

and install your in-law's couches. Worse,
they've saved the vision of the childhood
friend who lost a thumb and finger to the ax
she found behind your father's tool shed.
Girlish digits separate by the blade, her pink
face draining, and the minutes after—
screams turned inside out, the sock you used
to try to staunch the bleeding: these in all
their gore for months beside your pillow
like what a cat drops crippled on a threshold.

But it's not spitefulness why they cache
and disarticulate, why they pack your fragile
keepsakes in the kneelers overnight.
And not an arbitrary shuffling of your life
they practice like malicious solitaire.
No, they're priests who lack a scripture,
and this is how they've learned to worship
in the tall brick church that shadows you.
For a while one set of rituals was working.
Now they need others. Hence the ax
and couches. At times a stained glass
window is commissioned for a feast day
and for a while some cherished fire
will crackle in your head the way it used to.
Foolish though, to think the god they praise
is your biography. You're architecture
and artifact and they will whittle you down
to relics. Your purpose is to call the tips
of fingers holy, to let the tinctured sun fall
on whatever they place at the altar, to pray,
when you pray, from any pew they choose.

LULLABY WITH BOURBON

Behind you lie a hundred yards of satin
      paid out in a thin line,
trailed around the house in slinky corkscrews,
      tangled in the Ficus
like a kite. Now your knees need rest, your eyelids.
      Just sit a second,
Red Dress. Our guests are gone. Let's spool
      the evening's ravel back
around you. I'll look to the dishes while you swirl
      a splash of whiskey.

The hardest task for fantasists is clearly hosting
      realist parties,
pairing romance with meatloaf on a budget of nothing,
      playing wit and waitress
to our fete-starved friends. Your grace could make
      a hospital hospitable,
but while others convalesce, you worry at some flaw.
      Even now you hold
the bourbon like a handrail. Red Dress, it's designed
      to let you fall.

In the thrift of this room where the glitz is kitsch,
      let us slide off
our seats like dolls. Tonight be big-eyed
      and porcelain
in an invincibly fabulous outfit. Stylish
      even wrinkled.
And if Saturday's not washed and pressed for us
      like laundry,

let it come without that pomp
    and starch.

You are cordially invited to lie down the way
    a caravan of camels
hauling bolts of velvet through the jostled night
    lies down inside
their drivers' cadenced singing. You're invited
    to be bright
and poor and young. Now invite me
    to kiss you
with our eyes closed. Red, I can taste Kentucky
    on your tongue.

REVEILLE WITH LULLABIES

When we leave the house our son is crying
in his grandma's arms we leave him crying

From our loath retreat to the old drive-in
we call home and hear his crying
high and ragged through the phone

The credits cry and we speed back
as lightning cracks the wide horizon

From our garage we hear him crying
cribbed he cries his shrill alarms
though nothing breaches nothing's burning

Eventually we sleep or try
but cries outstrip the storm outside
that turns and turns our breathless beech

He screams and cries and chokes on crying
till the wall clock's black-lipped O
is crying back without a sound

The sleet-lined wind is crying too
its slats of streetlight through the blinds

And down the highway teams of sirens
Doppler by to brief our rooms
in cries of red and blue

* * *

If the colic were a creature,
thirsty in our son,
then you might sate it
with your cool wet voice,
your milky teaspoons of song.
You might reason with it,
you might coax it out
with singing, if the hurt
were conscious,
if the colic were a creature.

You vine your melody
around him as if to leach
the poison out and make
of it a full white flower
that could lure a moth
out of the night,
a moth to drink and take
the colic off beyond
the reaches of these limbs
you vine in melody.

Our son looks at your song
the way that birds look
into windows at a lie of clouds
they cannot comprehend.
As though his ears
were only mirrors, your voice
wrecks against his hearing,
falls, and then blinks long
into the dark the way
our son looks at your song.

Beyond his stream
of vowels something vicious

sings; it whistles in his lungs.
You listen and coo louder,
and now the colic hears
you coming. It knows
your gleaming tongue
and knows as well you mean
to drown it in the song
your vowels stream.

* * *

Tonight the drive-in featured a cry film.
For an hour stars and starlets jerked our tears.
A mom collided with a boy cashier
and both died in their cars beneath the elms
that lined the avenue with lush aplomb.
We watched the ruptured families in the year
that followed bleed and scab and volunteer
fresh traumas to re-mourn and re-embalm.

The incidental plot found little to pursue,
but the leads could act and we believed their grief.
As the daughter and her boyfriend screwed,
she cried against his shoulder: we cried too.
At jokes, the dad's sad laugh was no relief.
With him we smiled and had our smiles abused.

While the film wept on, I slipped away to breathe
and find the desolate concessions stand.
The aisles of pickups and sedans were thinned
to shadows by a low-lit scene. A breeze
rose, then the massive screen behind me greased
the lot in light: I saw a couple pinned
together wipe their eyes as they held hands;
a fat man dabbed his moustache with his sleeve.

It's strange we sometimes drive out there to cry
for strangers. We have loved ones we owe tears.
Sure, in one tall cab I caught a swoon-proof
cowboy scoffing, but even his sneer lied,
Behind a coupe I paused at length to hear
a woman sobbing faintly through her moonroof.

* * *

O the infant's cries are hollow
and they're heated and prehensile

They're the beaks of red mosquitos
ten-yards long and tensile

The two of us are battered ears
now pinkly slapped and ringing

The two of us wear battered ears
distinctly chapped and stinging

And the infant's cries are geysers
spurting kerosene and diesel fuel

O the infant's cries are acrid
where they're pooling in the vestibule

Some cries sear behind our eyes
some pluck the smallest muscles

Some cries die beneath our skin
and dry inside like fossils

One recites the whole of history
and one reduces it to shreds

One cry spins us like rotisseries
in the big white furnace of our bed

* * *

Your sleep dismantled by your son's distress,
you've learned to wear his crying like a mantle.
You bless and bless him and his cries cry less.

The lights gone out, your singing lights a candle
deep and soft as what the reefs fluoresce
beneath their sheets of salt. To chorus you cancel

your sleep. Dismantled by your son's distress,
the night around you weeps. Your song's a thimble,
if the hour's small and sharp; it's your own rest

you stitch around his shoulders as he trembles.
Your blessings dress him and his cries cry less.
Though now you shiver, cry, your crying's simple.

His hurt's a puzzle though his sobs digress
to whimpers for a while. Exhausted, he samples
your sleep. Dismantled by your song, distress

still aches in pieces like a scree of trampled
shadows, shattered glass. You build a nest
of it. You make the fractured night a temple.

You bless and bless it and its cries. Cry less,
Madonna. Wet-nurse angels reassemble
our dismantled sleep. Their sums redress;
their breasts refresh us and our sighs sigh less.

* * *

Because there's not enough rest in the world
there's not and won't be enough waking

We rise when something calls us out of bed

Your song's not addressed to the dark
we wake in
or for you as you dress in the dark

Your song is a host and the guests
it takes in
are those darkness has taken apart

There's not enough blessed in the world
we wake in

But your chorus is vanilla
and its waves of fragrant vowels
bathe our names delicious in our ears

Rise now rise now and bless us
till our cries lie down cry less

Notes

Reveille on a Silent Whistle
This poem and the other reveilles and lullabies are dedicated to
Elisabeth Clark.

Cradles
This poem is dedicated to Enid Shomer.

A Stipulation
This poem takes its epigraph from James Merrill's "The Peacock."

Prodigalia
Luke 15:13: "Not long after that the younger son got together all he
had and set off for a distant country . . . "

The Picture of Little G. C. in a Prospect of Flowers
This poem's title alludes to Andrew Marvell's "The Picture of Little
T. C. in a Prospect of Flowers," and to John Ashbery's "The Picture
of Little J. A. . . . "

Whatever Burn This Be
This poem is dedicated to John Poch.